Starting Drawing

JASON BOWYER

Series Editor
Ken Howard

First published in 1988 by
Bloomsbury Publishing Limited
This edition published 1991 by
Magna Books, Magna Road, Leicester, UK, LE8 2ZH
Reprinted 1992
Produced by the Promotional Reprint Company Limited
Copyright © Swallow Publishing Ltd. 1988

Note: Throughout this book, American terms are signalled in
parenthesis after their British equivalents the first time in
each section they occur. In frame and artwork measurement,
height always precedes width.

ISBN 1 85422 184 1

Printed and bound in Hong Kong

Contents

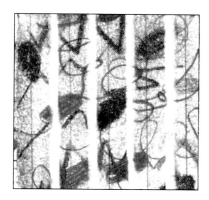

Foreword

'Why have I never seen that before?' These words were said to me many years ago by a man who had paused on his way to work for a few moments to watch me draw. Although he made that journey through the same landscape every day, it seemed that for the first time he had seen the view that had been before his very eyes all along. This process of opening people's eyes is one of the great values of drawing and painting.

In addition to opening other people's eyes, it is equally important to open one's own eyes. Drawing is a way of seeing. By that I mean drawing from nature actually makes you see nature, it opens your eyes to the world around you.

Drawing, like writing, has a grammar. Just as writing is made up of the letters, words, sentences and paragraphs, drawing is made up of marks, lines, shapes and tones. When we are young we learn to write through practice and through practice we develop our own handwriting; so too drawing demands practice and through that we develop our own style.

Ken Howard 'Interior: The Old Fulham Hospital 1971' 254 × 406mm (10 × 16in.) tonal wash.

Art Class is a series of titles geared specifically to the requirements of the amateur artist. While some of the books are subject-based, others are technique-based to help readers acquire first the basic, then the more advanced, techniques they need to enable them to work in a particular medium. All are full of sound practical advice, and suggest exercises and projects which readers can do in order to gain a clear understanding of the subject. All the writers involved in the series, as well as being professional artists, have at some time in their careers been involved in teaching in art schools.

Jason Bowyer's book is a coherent introduction to the elements of drawing. Reading it is the equivalent of being invited into a foundation drawing studio in an art school. Starting with advice on materials and organizing a work space, he considers the most basic of questions such as whether one should stand up or sit to work and how to make marks with pencils, ink and charcoal. He then takes us step by step through projects in various media and opens our eyes to ideas for subjects to draw.

This is a book full of sound practical advice as well as enthusiasm for drawing. Read it, assimilate it and you will find the enthusiasm catching and come to enjoy that exciting activity which is drawing.

Ken Howard

Jason Bowyer 'Jimmy's Boat' 175 × 228mm (6¾ × 9in.) charcoal.

4

Introduction

Drawing is the simplest and oldest art form. Drawn images are created by adults and children of all ages, in order to express feelings, communicate ideas to others, or simply for pleasure and the exhilaration of the act. Drawing is practised using different methods and materials, and in various forms in every culture and society throughout the world. Whatever the tools, whether pencil, charcoal, ink or pastel, all drawings are executed either in line or tone (or both). Line drawings are made purely in lines, whereas tone involves shading and degrees of light and dark.

The ability to draw and communicate through drawn marks is not a talent possessed by only a few people, but can be embraced by everyone with a little effort. This book will provide you with only a fraction of the enormous vocabulary of techniques and materials used in drawing. It is not the definitive book, but will show you one way to approach your first steps in drawing. At the heart of the book lies the belief that the person starting to draw must begin by observing the world around them before embarking on problems of expression.

"... and every day I am more convinced that people who do not first wrestle with nature never succeed."

Van Gogh, Nuenan, January 1885

This is how I started to draw myself. Seated at the kitchen table, working in pencil from observation, I learned the rudiments of measurement and simply got on with it. One of my earliest subject matters was a mound of potato peelings. It became an exciting wriggling pattern once I started to draw and observe.

"... Now hardly a day passes that I do not make something. As practice makes perfect, I cannot but make progress; each drawing one makes, each study one paints, is a step forward."

Van Gogh, Denthe, October 1883

For this reason, the book is built around exercises which are designed to develop your visual vocabulary of marks, lines and tone. I hope you will gain confidence through these sections and be unafraid to make mistakes as you progress. The simple exercises will begin to develop your awareness of space around you and the scale of objects, you will then be able to learn how to work from observation and to produce drawings exploring measurement and proportion.

Vincent van Gogh 'La Crau from Mont Majour' (detail) 480 × 608mm (19¼ × 24⅓in.). Van Gogh achieves a unified and peaceful composition using short, staccato lines and dots in ink. He creates a vast panorama with varying tonal marks that recede from the denser marks of the foreground to the vague suggestion of the horizon line.

Peter Paul Rubens 'Cows' (detail) 340 × 522mm (13⅜ × 20½in.). This drawing uses a combination of brown sepia ink and dip pen. The delicate, flowing lines of the dip pen capture the movement of the cows. The small sketches around the main study emphasize Rubens' interest in analysing the changing forms of the cow.

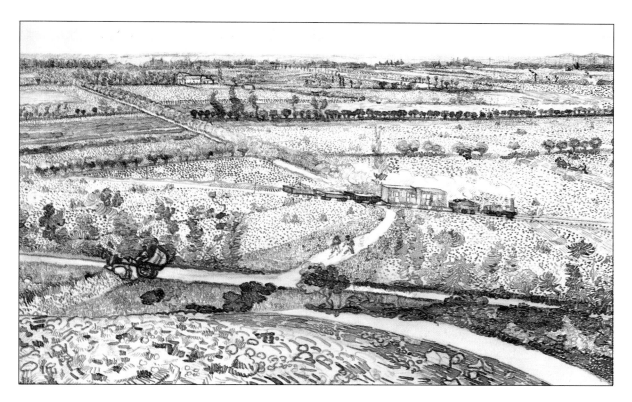

Materials, equipment and the workspace

You need only spend a little money to buy the simple materials needed to start drawing. There is, in fact, a wide variety of materials and equipment available, all of them with their uses, but only a selection of them is necessary for the beginner. To enable you to acquire equipment gradually, a list of materials is given wherever specific drawing projects are prescribed in this book, and you can just buy what you need for that type of drawing if you do not already have it.

The marks produced by different drawing media that are illustrated in this book are not to be taken as being definitive; they are merely examples of how to achieve various effects. It is important that you should develop your own way of working.

A selection of equipment from the kit recommended for the exercises and projects in this book.

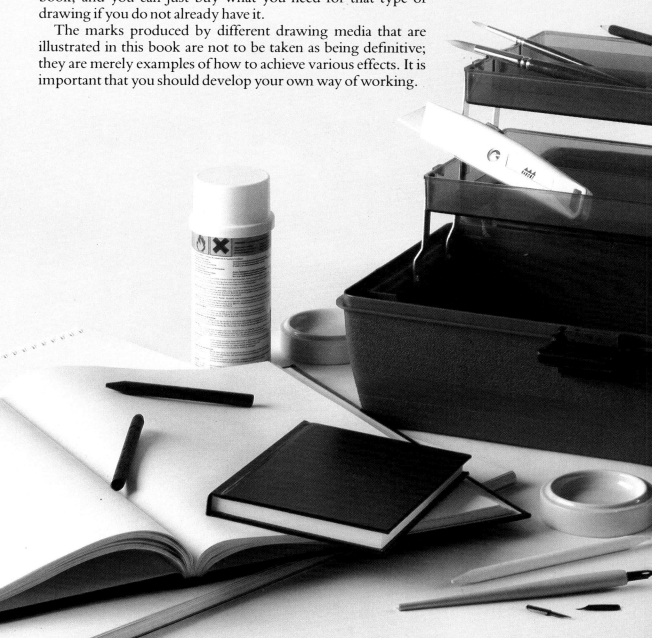

Recommended kit

The following pieces of equipment are easily available from art shops and hardware stores. The materials can be bought fairly inexpensively, especially if you shop around. With these you will be able to do the exercises and projects given in this book.

a plywood drawing board measuring 55 × 50cm (22 × 20in.)
white cartridge paper in different sizes
an A3 sketchpad of cartridge paper
a hardback sketchbook
2B, 4B and 6B pencils
a box of thick charcoal sticks, a few pieces of compressed charcoal and a soft charcoal pencil
a metal dip pen with a variety of nibs
a reed or bamboo pen
three nylon brushes
a plastic eraser
a bottle of Indian ink (waterproof)
a white oil crayon
a tube of white gouache
a plastic or ceramic stacking palette (cabinet nest)
a sharp craft knife such as a Stanley knife
a roll of masking tape or adhesive tape
a roll of gummed tape
rubber–based adhesive
a can of spray fixative
a metal ruler
a storage box

Basic equipment

Pencils

Pencil is a very popular medium due to its wide variety of uses in line drawing and tonal work, and its portability, which makes it ideal for impromptu sketching. It is probably also the tool that most readily comes to mind when people think of drawing. In artistic terms, however, the pencil is a relative newcomer, being invented by a Frenchman, Nicolas Jacques Conté, in 1795.

The central part of the pencil is made from carbon and clay. This part varies from hard to soft, and all pencils are graded accordingly. The harder ones range from H to 8H; the higher the number, the harder they are. Likewise with the soft ones, which start at B and go up to 8B. HB pencils are of intermediate hardness.

Hard pencils make a fine, sharp line, soft ones a dark line that can be sharp or soft, and are therefore more versatile in their use. Sharpened they make fine lines, rounded they produce soft, thick ones, and they are also useful in producing areas of tone. A good basic group to have is a range from soft to very soft, say a 2B, 4B and 6B.

Charcoal

Charcoal is the oldest drawing medium, and its origins probably go back to when the first cave-dweller picked a piece of burnt wood from the fire and started to make marks with it. When used for drawing it is shaped into sticks, or is in the form of a pencil. Like pencil, it can vary in hardness. Charcoal is often used to create tonal drawings because of the ease with which it can cover large areas.

Three types of charcoal are available:

Stick charcoal   This comes in a variety of thicknesses and lengths. Sometimes the sticks are sold separately but generally they are in a box containing 10 or 20. The thinnest sticks are usually used for line drawing. The thicker sticks are suitable for making tonal areas but can also be used for making a variety of lines.

Compressed charcoal   This comes in short sticks, and has a darker tone than stick charcoal. It is difficult to make a thin line with a piece of compressed charcoal unless it is sharpened but is very useful when you need a deep black tone to heighten the contrast in a stick charcoal drawing.

Charcoal pencils   These are graded extra soft, soft, medium and hard. They are used for line drawings and work well in quick sketchbook drawings. They are valuable when you need a sharp line to define the shape in a tonal stick charcoal drawing.

Paper

Paper is available in a range of sizes and surfaces. It is made from various combinations of wood fibre, flax, hemp and cotton. Sizes are identified by a coding system. The largest size ordinarily available is A1, measuring 841 × 594mm (33⅛ × 23⅜in.), the smallest A4, measuring 297 × 210mm (11¾ × 8¼in.).

The surface of paper can vary. Hand-made paper may have a textured surface or a smooth finish. A mass-produced paper will have a smooth finish. Papers made with a rag content make by far the most stable surface for your drawings, but can be prohibitively expensive. A simple A3 sketchpad of mass-produced cartridge paper, measuring 420 × 297mm (16½ × 11¾in.), will be perfectly adequate for the beginner.

Pens

Pens have been used for drawing since the early Middle Ages. They are commonly used by designers and draughtsmen, as well as by fine artists. Ink gives a darker, firmer line than pencil, the thickness of the line being determined by the fineness of the nib.

Reed and bamboo pens   Soft-wooded pens do not have any kind of canal or storage chamber to hold ink in, and therefore have to be dipped into ink frequently. The line that they create is usually rich and thick, varying according to the way the nib is cut.

Quill pens The quill feathers of birds, sharpened to a point, are often used for drawing with. Only naturally discarded feathers are suitable as they have to have attained sufficient maturity. The line created is elegant, and this makes them popular for calligraphy.

Metal dip pens The metal nibs which you insert into wooden or plastic pen holders come in varying thicknesses. These nibs retain a certain amount of ink, and so they do not have to be dipped too often.

Reservoir and fountain pens The reservoir pen has interchangeable nibs and is used by graphic and commercial artists. The ordinary fountain pen does not produce the versatility of line that is useful for the beginner to explore, and so is not generally recommended.

Initially you need only a wooden pen holder and a range of different thicknesses of nib. It would be useful, however, to have either a reed or bamboo pen.

Brushes

A pen and brushes that can be used together can create exciting marks and are especially valuable in doing tone work. Your basic drawing equipment should include brushes made from nylon fibre or nylon with a mix of sable. A size 2 round-ended, a size 7 round-ended and a size 8 flat-ended are a good basic set to begin with. With these brushes you will be able to work in line as well as create tonal washes for your drawings.

Ink

The first inks were made from candle soot and gum water in ancient China; they came in a solid form and were mixed with water. The Chinese used them for writing and drawing. Modern drawing inks like Indian ink (more often known as India ink in the USA) are made from gas black in aqueous adhesive; the addition of shellac soap makes them waterproof. Indian ink is excellent for drawing with, particularly for beginners because it is readily available and easy to manipulate.

Drawing board

It is essential to have a drawing board as this gives you a firm surface to work on. The best type of drawing board for the beginner is one made of light plywood measuring approximately 55 × 50cm (22 × 20in.). Your local timber merchant can cut you a board to size.

Erasers

The first erasers were made of either soft leather or freshly baked bread, but the discovery of rubber and the development of plastic have resulted in these crude forms of erasers dying out. Plastic erasers are excellent for pencil and charcoal. However, erasing ink is difficult, and commercial erasers cannot cope. The best way is to scrape the surface of the paper lightly with a sharp craft knife or a scalpel (X-acto knife). To get a sharp edge to a plastic eraser, cut with a sharp knife periodically.

Fibrous paper sticks commonly known as paper stumps (stomps) and properly called tortillon, are useful for spreading charcoal.

Other equipment

Charcoal and soft pencil will smudge quite easily if not treated, so fixatives are available which make dry mediums more permanent on paper. They come in the form of spray-on liquid. Instructions for use are always given on the side of the container and should be followed carefully.

Artists' oil crayons are impervious to water and are used when working in mixed media.

Cutting tools are essential for sharpening pencils and for cutting paper or card. A sharp craft knife is ideal for both of these tasks.

Drawing pins and masking tape are needed to attach paper to a drawing board or to put newly made drawings on the wall.

A metal ruler at least 30cm (12in.) in length is helpful both for cutting card and for marking out areas to draw in.

Finally, a storage box such as an old tool box or a plastic art bin is useful for organizing your equipment and keeping it together.

Recommended furniture (from left to right): a table, drawing board, chair, box easel, sketching easel, and radial easel.

Furniture

Table   You are going to need a table both to work at and to rest your drawing board against. It should be at a comfortable height.

Chair   A good kitchen chair without arms and giving your back support is essential for drawing in a seated position. A stool placed beside you is often useful for materials.

Easel   An easel is not essential when you are starting to learn to draw providing that you have a drawing board. If, however, you do have one it will give you a vertical surface to work on. You can either sit comfortably at arm's length from your board or stand to draw if your subject matter is on a shelf. The benefit of standing is that you can view your work from a varying distance more easily. This gives the eye a chance to scan the whole of the drawing. The proportions will become clearer to you: the size and scale of objects in relation to one another can be understood and altered.

There are three varieties of easel:

Radial easel   Commonly used in art schools, it is a large piece of equipment and hence not suitable for the average home.

Sketching easel   A collapsible easel that can easily be stored in a cupboard.

Box easel   A collapsible easel that folds down into and around the main box support. A useful, more stable version of the sketching easel.

Setting up

A little effort given to setting up will give you the chance to use your precious time more profitably. Looking for a missing pencil or eraser is frustrating and destroys your creative urge, leaving you exasperated and in no frame of mind to concentrate. It is best, therefore, to have everything you will need to hand when you start.

If you don't have anywhere you can use as a small permanent workspace, store all your materials in an art bin or tool box. Keep them in separate compartments so that you can find them without having to rummage around.

Organizing a small space

If possible, use part of a room permanently as your art area. An hour or two spent initially in arranging furniture, obtaining materials and organizing lighting will ultimately give you more time to draw. In deciding upon a desirable space, consider these points:

Light   It's important to choose somewhere with good, constant light – a space near a window, not a badly lit corner. You may want to work at night, so also make sure that you have sufficient artificial light to avoid straining your eyes.

Noise   Obviously, it's difficult to concentrate with constant noise and people moving around. Try to find a place where you will not be continually disturbed.

Heat   You may need to use your space in the winter for drawing. Find a place that has adequate heating. It's not advisable to have your space right next to a radiator as the heat would adversely affect the paper and art materials.

Sitting and standing to draw

Standing   Work at arm's length; it is impossible to get the proportions right if you work too close to the paper. It is a good idea to have a stool close by so that you can sit down occasionally to rest your legs, while you contemplate your work from a different position.

The author standing to draw.

Sitting   Most people find that sitting is more comfortable for drawing than standing, and certainly with most drawings there is no reason why you should not sit down. The important thing is that you have a good view of both your subject matter and your drawing board.

Choose a chair that gives your back support, then lean your drawing board on the edge of the table at an angle of 45 degrees so that it can rest easily on your lap. Try not to slouch or lean on your board as you draw. It is important to move away from your board at intervals of about 30 minutes so as to view your work from a distance. This enables you to check that the proportions are correct and that the tones work together as a whole. But do not move your chair or your subject, as when you sit down again you need to see what you are drawing from the same angle and position.

The author sitting to draw.

Stretching paper

When you come to draw with washes (pen and ink), you will need to be able to stretch the paper first. This is a way of wetting the paper and letting it dry so as to prevent it from wrinkling as the ink dries. The procedure is not as difficult as you might think and can be learned quickly.

If you are going to use your actual drawing board, keep to one side only, so you can preserve the other as a clean drawing surface. If you prefer, keep a separate board just for stretching paper. This will enable you to prepare paper and continue with other drawings at the same time.

First, place the paper in the centre of the board. Measure four lengths of gummed tape for the sides of the paper, making them slightly longer so they will overlap at the corners. Put these aside.

Then, gently dampen the surface of the paper with a sponge, turn the paper over, and repeat the process. Make sure the sponge is not too saturated with water – squeeze it out lightly before you start. Take care not to rub too hard as you could damage the surface of the paper.

Now fix the paper to the board. Run a strip of gummed tape under the tap (or through a dish of water) and lightly pull it through your fingers and thumb to get rid of the excess water (but do not remove the gum from the surface). Place the strip of tape along one edge of the paper so that half the width is over the paper and half is over the board. Repeat with the remaining strips of tape.

As you fix the tape, wipe along its edges with the sponge to absorb any excess water, and to make sure it is flat and has stuck all the way round. Do the same over the surface of the paper but just dabbing gently.

Allow the paper to dry at room temperature. Keep the board flat so the paper can dry evenly. Do not attempt to speed up the process by using a fan heater or by putting it beside a radiator as this would probably make the paper tear or buckle. When the paper is dry, it should be completely flat and ready to use.

HOW TO STRETCH PAPER

After placing your paper in the centre of the board, measure the four lengths of gummed tape to be slightly longer than each side of the paper (in order to overlap at the corners).

Using a sponge that is wet but not saturated, dampen the surface of the paper evenly to relax the fibres in the paper. Then turn the paper over and dampen the other side.

Wet the gummed tape by either running it under a tap or through a dish of water, gently taking off the excess water with your fingers and thumb.

Having fixed the gummed tape along the four edges of the paper in such a way that half of the tape width is over the board, wipe off any excess water with the sponge.

Basic line techniques

Line drawing is simply the drawing of shapes with lines only, without any shading or tone. It is the most basic form of drawing, and as such is the foundation for every other technique. However, this does not mean that it is somehow inferior to other forms of art, for line on its own provides enormous scope. Look at the different types of line that are all around you: the sharp, straight line of a window, the curved lines of a cup, or the crinkly edge of a fern, for example.

The initial step when approaching drawing for the first time is to investigate the varieties of line made by the different media so as to become familiar with them before working from observation.

You will need
☐ a drawing board
☐ A3 sheets of paper
☐ 2B, 4B and 6B pencils
☐ a dip pen, nibs and ink
☐ brushes
☐ a plastic eraser
☐ a ruler
☐ masking tape
☐ a sharp craft knife
☐ a stacking palette (cabinet nest)
☐ a container of water

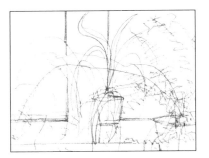 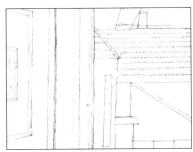

Far left: The sharp, straight lines of the window frame make a stark contrast to the zig-zagging, curling plant leaves.
Left: View through a window showing the different weights of line in the architecture of the buildings and the various angles that they make.

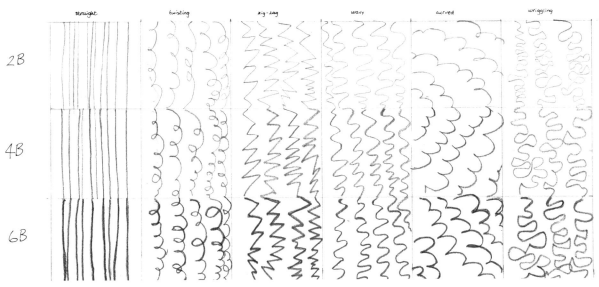

Lines in pencil – the finished exercise.

Lines in pencil

Always sharpen your pencils with a sharp craft knife or scalpel (X-acto knife). This gives you a much stronger point and is less wasteful of the pencil than using a pencil sharpener.

Attach the sheet of paper to the drawing board horizontally, and mark out a box measuring 15 × 30cm (6 × 12in.). Divide the box into 50mm (2in.) squares. Write the number of each of the different grades of pencil you are using down the left-hand side, next to the first three squares. Below each vertical line of boxes, write a different word to describe a type of line: for example, straight, twisting, zig-zag, wavy, curved, wriggling.

Start in the top left-hand corner box and fill it with lines according to the type you have chosen, using a 2B pencil. When you reach the bottom edge of that box, change to a 4B pencil and continue down, connecting the lines. Change to a 6B box for the bottom box. As you use the various grades of pencil, try different pressures on the point to see the different density of line. The greater the pressure, the darker the line will be.

Lines in dip pen and brush

On an A3 sheet of paper, attached vertically to the drawing board, mark out a box measuring 30 × 15cm (12 × 6in.) with a pencil and ruler. Mark out two lines at 50mm (2in.) intervals, running from top to bottom. Measure 50mm (2in.) down from the top of the box and mark out two lines 12mm (½in.) apart running horizontally across the paper. Measure another 50mm (2in.) from the lower line, and then draw another two horizontal lines 12mm (½in.) apart. Proceed in this way down the paper until you reach the bottom of the box.

In each of 12mm (½in.) wide spaces beneath the boxes, write a word describing the type of line that you are trying to create. Write underneath the box for the bottom three squares. Then draw these lines in the boxes with Indian ink, using both different nib widths and brushes. You should try to make each line or group of lines within each box contrast with the next one. One way of achieving this contrast is to experiment with different nibs and brushes.

When you are making lines inside the boxes, try not to use a ruler; it is better to work freehand. Be patient about your ability to manoeuvre the pen or brush and don't worry about smudges.

Lines in dip pen and brush – the finished exercise.

Working from observation

By practising drawing different lines in pencil, dip pen and brush, you will begin to have an understanding of materials and their effects. Next is to learn how to look. The first exercise to develop the skill of co-ordinating your eye and your hand is to make a series of small line drawings in pencil and dip pen from observation. At this stage the question of proportion need not worry you. Just respond to what you see in front of you, the shape and movement of the line. These are your first tentative steps in observational drawing, so the results might seem rather limited but don't be discouraged.

Looking at straight lines

New students often complain of not being able to draw a straight line. Indeed, drawing straight lines freehand does take practice, but the following exercise will help. It will also start you looking properly at angles.

Attach an A3 sheet of paper horizontally to the drawing board. Draw a line down the middle of the paper in pencil. Work on either side of this line, alternating your drawings in dip pen with your drawings in pencil. If your pen seems to be clogging up with ink and not making a steady line, clean it in water.

Look at the top right-hand corner of the drawing board; you are now going to draw that angle. Make a dot on the paper (on the right-hand side) to represent the point where the two edges of the board meet. Look along the top line of your board and place another dot on the paper, about 75mm (3in.) to the left of the first. Now look down the right-hand side of the board and place a dot on the paper, about 75mm (3in.) below the original dot. Join the three dots, and you should have an angle of approximately 90 degrees.

This method of line construction gives points of reference as you plot angles and create straight lines. It is a good basis for building up an image on paper from observation.

Look around you in the room and draw different angles, either using the dot-line method to plot angles or just trying to draw straight lines from observation. It is difficult to draw a straight line longer than 15cm (6in.) If, however, you first make a series of dots at 75mm (3in.) intervals, it becomes easier. Fill the two halves of the A3 sheet with studies of angles and straight lines.

When you are working from observation, you should always glance from the subject to the drawing repeatedly and quickly.

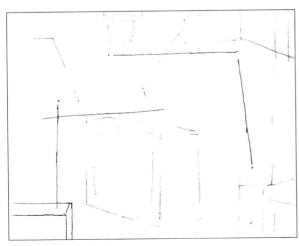

Drawing straight lines.

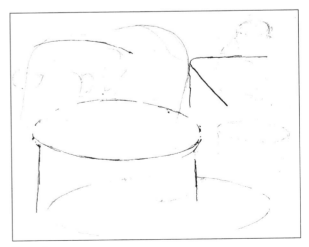

Drawing curves.

Looking at curves

Attach an A3 sheet of paper horizontally to the drawing board. Arrange an assortment of cups, saucepans, and other items that have simple curves, in front of you.

Using a dip pen and pencil alternately, create a series of curves based on those in the objects in front of you. As in the previous exercise, remember to keep glancing at the object and back to the paper. Try to draw each curve in an unbroken line without removing your pen or pencil from the paper, varying the shapes and sizes of the curves according to the objects in front of you. At first your curves may not flow smoothly, but you should soon be able to draw a curve with a single stroke of the pen or pencil.

After a number of attempts, when you feel more satisfied with your efforts, look around you in the room for any other curves such as the side of a fruit bowl or a lamp base and stand.

In the case of a more complex or larger curve, try drawing it by the dot-line method that you used to draw straight lines. Mark three dots, the middle one at the highest point of the curve and the others at either end. Join them together, again glancing at the object and back to the paper to help you get the right shape.

Looking at crumpled paper

The edge of a piece of crumpled paper has a combination of different lines. In some places it is straight; in others it can be crinkly. Drawing the outline of the paper, with these different lines is a good test of the skills you have started to develop.

Divide an A3 sheet of paper with a pencil line down the middle and attach it horizontally to the board. Then crumple an A4 piece of paper, so you have a shape that has a series of different contours. Place it on the table in front of you, preferably on a darker background.

Attempt to follow the line of the contours of the crumpled paper by observation and convey this on one half of the A3 paper in pencil or ink. You should try to make the density of line delicate, by varying the pressure on the point of the pencil or pen.

Change the shape or position of the crumpled piece of paper to get a different edge for each drawing on the two halves of the paper.

Drawing crumpled paper is a demanding exercise, so you will need to persevere. You could also try drawing other crumpled objects like cushions or a pile of washing. The line of your non-drawing hand is another interesting subject as it can take so many different positions.

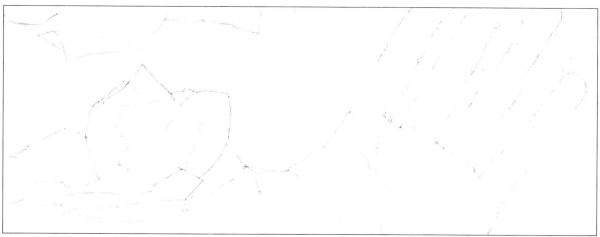

A drawing of crumpled paper and the author's non-drawing hand.

Measurement and proportion

Perspective is a means of representing three-dimensional forms on a two-dimensional surface. The theory is the most difficult prospect for people starting to draw from observation, but it is essential to grasp in order to do representational drawings. The basic rules were developed during the early Italian Renaissance, and are still used today.

Right: Interior of the Kew Bridge Steam Museum. Using sight-size measurement as a framework, I worked in Indian ink to create a tonal perspective of the architecture and machinery.

Measurement techniques

The practical process of sight-size measurement is the simplest way to teach yourself how to understand perspective. Sight-size means that the object should be the same size as it would appear to be if the paper were transparent and you simply traced the object on it at arm's length.

Look around your room and try this little experiment. Place a bottle 2 metres (6ft) away from you, at eye level; hold a pencil at arm's length and measure the bottle's height against the length of the pencil with one eye closed. Now place the bottle 4 metres (12ft) away and measure it again in the same way. The bottle should be considerably smaller against the length of the pencil.

The main principle of perspective is that the further away objects are, the smaller they appear to the eye. This is immediately discernible by sight-size measurement.

Before you start to measure an object, you should consider the following important points:

Position   Keep the same position in relationship to the object. While measuring, hold your head at the angle you wish to draw at.

Eyes   Look at an object in front of you with your left eye closed, then open your left eye and close your right. Repeat this procedure a few times in quick succession. The object jumps from side to side.

Arm   When you measure, keep your arm fully extended and straight.

Pencil   Keep your pencil vertical while measuring. Imagine that there is a pane of glass at arm's length and hold your pencil against it.

Accuracy   Try to be correct, but bear in mind that total precision is not possible. The sight-size system will help give your observational drawing a simple structural base, but is not meant to produce mathematical accuracy.

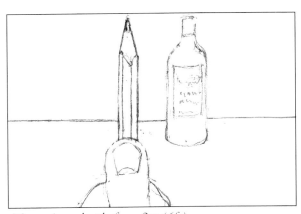

Measuring a bottle from 2m (6ft).

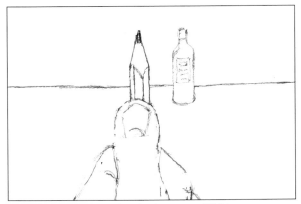

Measuring the same bottle from 4m (12ft).

Drawing an object sight-size

Place a cup 15cm (6in.) beyond arm's length on a table. Measure the cup's height with your arm extended, one eye closed and your pencil vertical.

Mark the top point of the rim of the cup on the paper; do the same with the bottom point of the cup to the distance indicated by your pencil.

Next, measure the distance from the mark you have made for the top of the rim to the lowest point of the rim, and mark it. You should now have three marks directly in line with one another. Draw a straight line through these marks.

To work out the width of the cup, measure horizontally across it from rim to rim. Place two marks to represent these points on the drawing. Draw a straight line extending horizontally through these marks.

Join the marks with curves to create the rim of the cup. When drawing curves, remember to move your eyes from drawing to object quickly – look and draw. The rim is now complete.

To draw the sides of the cup, measure them by sight, make two marks and connect. Draw the bottom of the cup in the same way.

Next draw the handle of the cup by measuring the top, bottom and side points of the handle, make three marks and then connect them, using the scanning process described above.

Look at the inside of the handle and draw its shape in relationship to the outside edge.

Finally, draw the table edge behind the cup, measuring the distance from the top of the rim.

Now repeat the drawing, this time placing it 45cm (18in.) beyond arm's length. Compare the size of the cup in your first and second drawings. This will demonstrate clearly how objects appear smaller as they move further away from you.

When connecting your marks, try to use them only as general reference. You should look from the object to your drawing, scanning the images swiftly rather than pondering. In this way, comparisons of the marks and actuality can be made more efficiently.

Joining the first three marks that indicate the rim.

Drawing a straight line across the cup's width.

Drawing the rim of the cup with curves.

The sides and bottom edge of the cup drawn in.

Putting in the cup handle, after measuring it.

After measuring the distance from the top point of the rim to the table edge, the line of the table edge is drawn.

Drawing a group of objects

When you draw a combination of objects, the spaces between them are just as important as the outline of each item and its proportions. You should treat each object as part of the group. In this way you are better able to involve the relationship between each item, which is very important in terms of creating a cohesive scale drawing. In the early stages of such a drawing, you should try to get used to leaving the objects in an unfinished form.

In this exercise you should measure both the objects and the spaces between them to sight-size.

Place a group of four objects on a table in front of you. The objects should include a cylinder (for example, a tall glass, an aerosol can, or a tube container of talcum powder), a sphere (a tennis ball, a softball, or an orange), an angular or curved shape (a pepper mill, a large perfume bottle, or a sauce bottle), and an irregular sphere (a large potato, stones or large pebbles). The objects should not be higher than 20cm (8in.) and not

smaller than 75mm (3in.) Arrange them as shown, with the cylinder in the centre.

Make a mark with a 2B pencil for the top left-hand point of the cylinder in the top centre of the paper (point A). Measure the distance using sight-size to the irregular sphere below. Make a mark (point B), then draw a line between the two marks. From point B, measure across to the far right-hand side of the regular sphere, make a mark and draw part of its curve. This is point C.

Now, to work out the horizontal dimension, from point B to the far left-hand side of the angular shape. This is point D, mark and draw part of its edge. If the table edge crosses the AB line, measure from point A and draw it in.

Again, measure horizontally from point B across to the other side of the cylinder. As this is obscured by the sphere, you will have to judge its position and make a mark. Draw the line of the cylinder. Measure diagonally downwards from point C to the far left-hand edge of the irregular sphere. Mark this point E and draw part of its edge on your drawing.

The objects arranged on a table.

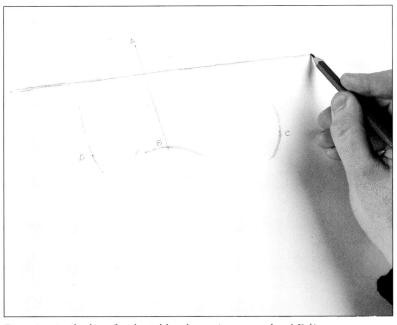

The first lines emerging.

Drawing in the line for the table edge as it crosses the AB line.

Measure diagonally upwards from point E to the top left–hand point of the angular shape (point F). Mark and draw part of its edge. From point F, measure to the highest point of the cylinder and draw its top curve.

Now that you have drawn the basic framework of the objects, start to measure and look at them individually. Draw their outlines. Measure the distances between shapes that are next to each other and mark them. Keep the drawing simple, concentrating on the outlines of the objects.

Finally, draw the contour lines on the objects. At this stage, stick to lines and do not worry

Putting in the irregular curves of the potato.

Drawing the top curve of the cylinder.

Giving the objects their simple outlines.

about tone. Make marks, shapes and lines that suggest the objects' form. Use an eraser to clarify your drawing where necessary, and to remove the lines that run through the objects.

If you have to leave the drawing unfinished for a few days, mark the positions of the objects on the table with masking tape (alternatively, you could place a sheet of paper under the objects when setting the group up, and draw round them to mark their position on this). Try to leave your chair in the same position, or make a note of exactly where you placed it, so that when you come back you will be in the same position in relation to the objects.

Finally, making marks, shapes and lines that suggest the objects' forms.

Further ideas

Enlarging and reducing

The process of sight-size measurement creates a framework and guidelines for you to work within. If you want to make a drawing that is larger than sight-size, start by measuring the objects sight-size, but then double the measurements. The same process can be used to reduce the image: measure the objects to sight-size, but then halve the measurements. These techniques of enlarging and reducing a scene are useful when you need to work on a small scale or want to cover a larger area.

Format

A simple method of extending your understanding of measurement and proportion is to change the format and size of your paper. Cut an A3 sheet of cartridge paper into different-sized squares, rectangles and circles. Make drawings in outline that cover the whole of each piece of paper. On a thin, horizontal rectangular shape, for instance, you could draw a slice or section only of a scene, such as the shopping arcade (mall) I drew. On the round piece I chose a flower to echo the format. You could also use different measurements: sight-size, half sight-size or twice sight-size.

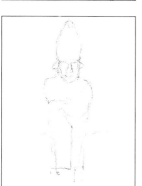

As an exercise in understanding format and measurement I drew a series of different subjects on different shaped pieces of paper. The study of a figure in a landscape was done sight-size; the scene of the shops and the doorway drawings were made to half sight-size; the flower and the figure were twice sight-size.

Tonal techniques

Line is a very beautiful medium to work in on its own, but its representational range can be enhanced by combination with tone. Tone is the world of colour represented in black and white. To show mass, tonal areas have to be drawn, and the graduations of light and dark need to be realized.

Before you start to work on a tonal drawing, make this simple comparison. Switch on your television set, and if it is colour turn down the brightness and turn up the contrast. You should see a limited image that seems to be essentially only light and dark. As you look at the image, increase the brightness. The greys should start to appear, creating more definition and more intricate forms.

Now go and sit a few paces away from a window. Slowly close your eyes until you are squinting. You should see a limited image with great contrast, like the television screen without the brightness. As you slowly open your eyes, the forms will become more defined, and the variety of tones between light and dark will become greater. The eye can pick out many more tones than the television image.

As with the television, the materials used when drawing cannot define the range of tones that the eye perceives. The subtlety has to be simplified.

The tonal range picked out by the human eye.

Definition is reduced when squinting.

Dark to light and light to dark

As in line, the first step is to get accustomed to perceiving and representing linear shapes, so with tone, the first step is to become familiar with basic tonal techniques.

Attach an A3 sheet of paper to the board vertically. Mark a pencil line horizontally across the centre of the paper.

Mark 22 straight lines at 12mm (½in.) intervals, 25mm (1in.) above the central line. Write the letter D (for 'dark') underneath the first vertical channel. Mark the next channels, from left to right, 1 to 9. Mark the tenth channel L (for 'light'), the next channels 9 to 1 and the last D.

Using a pencil create a deep tone with heavy, merged marks in the first channel. Go on to the next channel, making the marks slightly less black. Continue until the middle channel which should be left clear. Then continue, making each channel to the right gradually darker again. The art is to judge it so as to achieve an evenness to the increasing lightness and darkness.

Using a pencil alone is very unlikely to produce accurate results. Work into the graduated channels with an eraser, lightening areas, or use a paper stump (stomp) to spread the carbon and create subtle tones. You can also use your fingers.

You may have to work up and down the series of channels, lightening or darkening as you go; this is quite acceptable, do not expect to get it right the first time.

Pencil

Pencil can be used to produce shading, and often is in a sketchbook. However, when you begin to look at tone, pencil gets you involved with drawing only small areas and detail, whereas one should first master overall tonal scale. Charcoal and ink are much better for this. When using pencil for tone you can use the edge of the lead as well as the point.

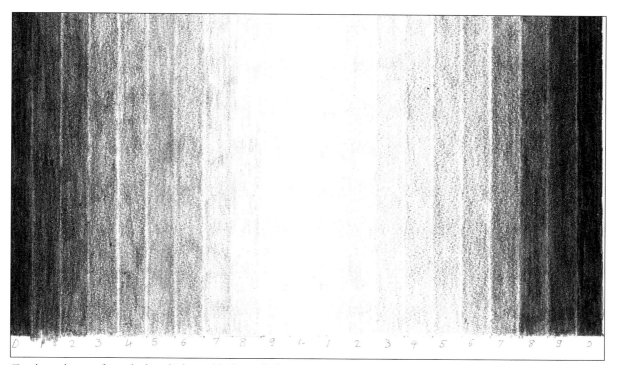

Graduated tones from dark to light and light to dark.

Using charcoal

Underneath your first tonal exercise in pencil, mark eleven 25mm (1in.) vertical straight lines, about 160 mm (6½ in.) high. Mark a straight diagonal line from the top left-hand corner to the bottom right-hand corner.

At the top left-hand corner above your first channel write the letter L, then write from 1 to 8 above the next eight channels and the letter D above the last channel. Write in the same letter and numerals, but in reverse order, at the bottom of the channels. The letter D denotes the darkest tone, the letter L the lightest tone.

This time build a series of tones in the top section above the diagonal line, working from light to dark in gradual steps with a stick of charcoal. In the section below the diagonal line, work from dark to light in gradual steps.

Although charcoal can be messy and difficult to preserve due to its powdery quality, its subtlety in tonal gradations is such that it is well worth persevering to learn how to use it. You may well need to use a paper stump or your fingers to spread the charcoal. A plastic eraser is useful to take away built-up tones of charcoal.

Using a paper stump to spread charcoal.

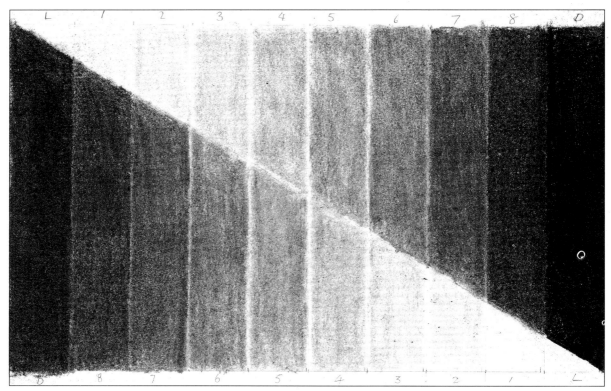

Tonal steps – the finished exercise.

Working with ink

Tone can be achieved with different intensities of ink. Pencil out a 25cm (10in.) square on an A3 sheet of paper. Draw a diagonal line from the top left-hand corner to the bottom right-hand corner, then draw another line from the top right-hand corner to the bottom left.

Mark six points at 25mm (1in.) intervals on each diagonal line starting from the central point. Connect the points with straight lines, creating a series of squares. You should be left with a border of 6mm (¼in.) on the outside.

Mark the central square D, denoting darkest. Number the outside squares from 1 to 5. Leave the remaining border completely clear.

Now take a plastic palette. To obtain the gradation of tones you need, put pure ink in one section. Put pure ink in the next section, but add a small quantity of water, progressively adding more water to each section until you have a series of different washes that become lighter.

Working flat on the table to prevent the ink running, use a brush to make the central square of your tonal square completely black with pure ink. As you work towards the outside of the subsequent squares, make each one slightly lighter by using a more diluted wash.

Use a flat-ended brush to make the washes. Work as swiftly as you can but try to keep the tones created by the brush even and straight. After each different square is completed, wash your brush in clean water and remove the excess water from the bristles with a tissue.

It takes time to learn how to make even washes. Initially, the effect of gradation from the black square in the centre to the white of the border is more important than an exact, smooth wash.

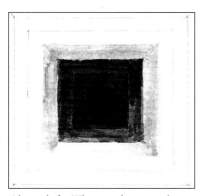

Above left: The tonal square drawn out; with some washes (below left); and completed (right).

Cutting the square notches in the top section.

Cutting the slits in the back section.

Making notches in one of the side sections.

Tonal theatre

A good way of learning to see how objects are made up of light and dark tone areas, is to use a tonal theatre or light modulator. The tonal theatre or light modulator is quite easy and quick to make and will help your appreciation of tone by confining your vision.

Making the tonal theatre

When cutting out card, always use a drawing board to protect the surface of the table. It is also helpful to have an extra strip of card under the area you are going to cut; this stops the knife embedding itself in the drawing board and prevents the surface from getting too many gouges. Always use a craft knife and a sturdy ruler to keep the cuts straight. Make sure the blade is sharp, but keep your fingers at a safe distance.

Place the card on the drawing board on a firm surface. Mark and cut out two rectangles measuring 32.5 × 25cm (13 × 10in.) and two rectangles measuring 27.5 × 25cm (11 × 10in.).

Place one of the larger rectangles on the drawing board. This will be the top section. Mark a 25mm (1in.) square in pencil in each corner. Cut these squares out with a craft knife.

Place the other larger rectangle on the drawing board vertically. This will be the back section. Draw lines horizontally right across the card with the ruler 25mm (1in.) in from both ends. Measure 40mm (1½in.) in at each of the four ends of the two horizontal lines and mark these points. The middle section of these lines should measure 17.5cm (7in.) Cut slits horizontally between these points with a craft knife as shown.

The sides of the tonal theatre are identical. Place one of the smaller rectangles on the board so that the 27.5cm (11in.) edges are at the top and bottom. On the right-hand side of the rectangle, mark and cut out two corner pieces 50mm (2in.) deep and 25mm (1in.) wide. Measure 50mm (2in.) down from the top of the card. Mark a line horizontally across the board. Measure 18mm

(¾in.) in to the left of the top corner point and to the right of the left-hand end, and cut slits along the horizontal line with a craft knife for the back section to slot into. Repeat the process with the other smaller rectangle to make the second side.

Assemble the tonal theatre by pushing the sides through the back slits. Then push the top through the side slits. Widen the slits if they are too tight to take the card.

Using the tonal theatre

When you have assembled your card theatre, place it on a table and put different objects inside. These should vary in their surface, shape and material. Try to imagine them as small sculptures. Look out for interesting things you could use: small artifacts, little boxes or anything that you may have collected on country walks or when beachcombing. You should choose a contrasting selection of objects; you can also try various combinations of articles in different positions. You could even make some objects yourself, or wrap some of the items in paper or material to disguise or soften the shapes.

Move the theatre around on the table so that you can see the variety of light and the way it falls inside the theatre.

You will find that by putting objects in this box you cut out distractions and can concentrate on their tonal features. Draw them in ink or charcoal.

Further ideas

When you have become familiar with the tonal theatre, you can experiment with different effects. To get different lighting on the objects inside it, cut shapes or slots in the top. Experiment with dramatic lighting effects at night by placing an angled desk lamp or a bedside lamp above the box. Make studies of different objects in charcoal; try to achieve a strong contrast of tone to match what you see. Also draw something in pencil, concentrating on just a section of the theatre rather than showing the whole thing.

Try also putting a mirror in the tonal theatre, either a piece of mirror specially cut to fit in, or a hand mirror. Place this mirror under a single object and do a drawing of it looking at the shape of both the object itself and its mirror image.

You can also create several small studies across one sheet of cartridge paper, changing the object every time you finish a drawing. Work on each drawing for no more than 15 minutes. You can achieve different effects by moving your theatre around to change the direction of the light.

Slotting the side piece into the back section.

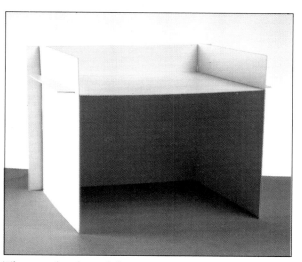

The completed tonal theatre.

Projects: Tonal drawings

This drawing will take you step–by–step through the process of working in charcoal from dark to light. Charcoal is often worked this way; it involves first covering the paper with a layer of charcoal, and then removing it in parts. The commentary is merely a guideline for you to follow, not the definitive method. Try to develop your own techniques for looking and working from ·my approach. As charcoal is difficult to manipulate on a small scale, it is often advisable to work larger than sight-size, as in this project.

A charcoal drawing

You will need
☐ a drawing board
☐ an A2 sheet of paper
☐ grey paper or card
☐ stick charcoal
☐ a charcoal pencil
☐ compressed charcoal
☐ a dip pen and nibs
☐ Indian ink
☐ brushes
☐ a paper stump (stomp)
☐ a plastic eraser
☐ masking tape
☐ spray fixative
☐ a ruler
☐ a soft rag
☐ a container of water

Above: I selected three objects for my arrangement that had a combination of contrasting lines. Left: The finished drawing.

Setting up the tonal theatre

The tonal theatre was set in front of me on a table. Underneath it I placed a piece of grey paper, allowing a distance of about 60cm (2ft) from the edge of my drawing board (when sitting in my drawing position) to where I placed the theatre. I then selected three objects from my collection of articles that I found interesting, and arranged them so that I would use the back, middle and front sections of the theatre.

Basic outline

After attaching to my drawing board a single A2 sheet of cartridge paper cut down to fit the board, I positioned myself directly in front of the theatre. The first job was to make a basic outline drawing using charcoal pencil of the frame of the theatre to twice sight-size. It was important to be as accurate as possible (within reason, of course) with the measurements, as this was the structure from which the tonal arrangement would emerge. The twice sight-size scale meant that I had to use a ruler as well as my pencil, to take the measurements with. I made a couple of small charcoal marks on the outside edges of my theatre drawing to indicate the main lines. These would be obliterated by the thick charcoal layer I was about to apply.

Establishing the lightest point

In order to get a clear idea of the strongest tones I looked at the objects inside the theatre with my eyes half closed, as if squinting in sunlight. The very lightest section, which was the crescendo of light in the theatre, was to be left completely free of charcoal in my drawing. Within the rest of the framework I applied a thick layer of stick charcoal, which I worked into the paper with bold strokes, creating a deep tonal layer of charcoal covering almost the entire frame of the theatre.

Creating mid-tone

I looked at the tonal theatre again with my eyes half closed. The back wall of the theatre seemed to be a mid-tone; certainly it was lighter than the floor of the theatre. Using a soft rag, I very lightly erased a layer of charcoal from the back wall of the theatre to create a mid-tone layer.

Starting on the objects

Taking a piece of compressed charcoal, which is darker than stick charcoal, I started to measure with a ruler and pencil and draw the outline of the objects inside the theatre to twice sight-size. I could quite easily see the shapes emerging from the stick charcoal layer. It is important that the measurements of the objects relate to each other and the frame of the theatre.

Light sections

With the lightest section of my drawing free from charcoal, I wanted to bring out the other light areas inside the tonal theatre. Again, I squinted, looking at the theatre to check the relative tonal values. Using a soft rag, I lightly erased a section

Drawing out the basic outline of the tonal theatre.

Covering almost the whole surface in charcoal.

Creating the mid-tones.

of the foreground of the theatre to indicate the light entering it. With an eraser I highlighted those parts of the roll of tape caught by the light (the sharp edge of a plastic eraser allows you to be more controlled and remove more charcoal).

Dark sections

I then had to put in the darkest lines and sections. The darkest areas seemed to be at the back edges of the theatre, around and in between the objects. I again used compressed charcoal to draw in these darkest sections. At this point in the drawing I knew the lightest and darkest parts of the drawing and had drawn them in. All the other tones had to be between these values.

Increasing definition

I stepped back and looked at the drawing from a distance. The drawing needed more mid-tones, so I worked these using a plastic eraser, a soft rag and sometimes my fingers. I also used the compressed charcoal to emphasize some lines and shadows. I assessed the tone by frequently glancing at the subject, then working on my drawing. The definition of the shadows around the objects became more obvious by the removal of a layer of charcoal from the objects themselves, and by application of the compressed charcoal. The process of removal of charcoal and adding to and slightly changing the lines using the charcoal pencil to create more exacting shapes was completed at this stage.

Finishing off

In this last step I used the plastic eraser to create sharp, light lines at the front corner of the theatre. Then with the stump (stomp) I merged and spread the mid-tones in the foreground and midground. I then decided that the drawing was finished, so I used a spray fixative (always follow the instructions carefully) to protect the drawing and prevent it smudging. You can use a soft rag gently to remove thin lines of charcoal if necessary before spraying a drawing with fixative.

Drawing the outline of the shapes against the charcoal background.

Removing a charcoal layer with an eraser.

Using compressed charcoal for the darkest sections.

Merging the mid-tones with a paper stump.

A drawing in pen and wash

Having worked from dark to light in the last drawing, this one uses mid-tones with washes and lines, working more from light to dark. Although one can work from light to dark with charcoal, it is the only way of working with ink washes as the ink, once applied, cannot be removed like unfixed charcoal. The method one uses will depend a little on the darkness desired for the end result, but is mainly determined by taste. Only towards the end of the drawing is the darkest tone established. The process of slowly creating a series of transparent tonal washes is an excellent starting point for anyone who wishes to paint in watercolour.

Do not forget the principles you have learned in measurement and proportion drawings; try to use them in conjunction with these new methods.

Arranging the composition

I set up the tonal theatre in the same position as for the charcoal drawing. The objects were arranged so that they overlapped but still filled the entire space of the theatre.

I then positioned myself directly in front of the theatre, resting the drawing board with stretched paper on my lap and against the edge of the table. I made a sight-size outline drawing of the frame of the theatre in soft charcoal pencil.

The arrangement of objects inside the tonal theatre.

The finished drawing in pen and wash.

Drawing the basic outlines of the objects.

Basic outline

Using charcoal pencil, I started to measure and draw the outline of the objects within the theatre. As I drew, I observed carefully the shapes between the objects as well as the objects themselves. I kept the lines faint as in the first step.

Drawing the mid-tones

Judging that this would be the number needed, I mixed four different washes in my stacking palette. They represented an even progression across the tonal scale; the last wash had just a touch of water added. It is important to test the strength of each wash in a corner of the stretched paper before applying it to the drawing. You can then lighten or darken the wash if it does not seem right. This testing is especially important in the later stages of a drawing when the scope for correction is less.

I looked at the darker and medium areas of the theatre and the objects using the technique of screwing up my eyes to determine their exact location. Then with a flat-ended brush I drew them all in a mid-tone wash. As I applied the washes, I kept looking at the subtle changes in the shapes of the objects in relation to the theatre, changing them as I wished. This was not just a matter of filling in the drawn-out spaces, but was crucial to the whole drawing. I then went over the darkest areas in a slightly darker wash.

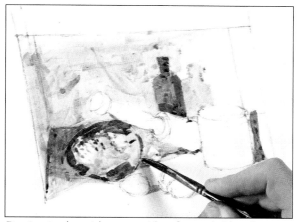
Putting in the mid-tones with a flat-ended brush.

The shapes emerge

Using a slightly lighter wash, I applied another layer of tone to the areas in the tonal theatre that appeared to use the next lightest once I had established a range of mid-tones in the drawing. I then felt ready to tackle the darker edges of the theatre and the objects, and drew them in with a dip pen. At this point in the drawing I was looking at the general shapes, and not getting involved with the patterns on the objects or with any detail.

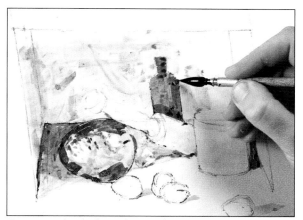
Drawing the darker edges in dip pen.

Achieving contrast

Some of the areas I had drawn in with mid-tone washes now seemed too light in contrast with the darker areas I had just drawn in, so I went over these in darker washes.

The darkest tones

In this final step, I washed in the darkest tones using my round-ended brushes. The washes very often overlapped and started to provide detail. The shadows became more defined; the feeling was that of looking at an entrance to an enclosure which was the effect I had been hoping to create. The final washes were added to create a strong contrast and I was now satisfied with the drawing.

Creating a contrast with the final, darkest washes.

Mixed media techniques

Drawing in mixed media might sound like a contemporary invention, but the process has in fact been around for centuries. Mixed media means using combinations of different materials together, such as pencil and ink. Exciting patterns and textures can be created as you experiment with different combinations of materials. These exercises will help you to explore the richness and variety of marks, lines and tone. You should try to make each one have an individual quality; you aren't just doodling, you are exploring a vocabulary for future drawings.

Guidelines are given in each of the different exercises as to how to create the marks, but they are only suggestions and you should follow them loosely. It is important to create your own qualities and to be prepared to combine the unexpected and the accidental in these exercises.

Degas 'Ballet Dancers' (detail) 473 × 625mm (19 × 25in.). A quick study in line on toned paper captures the dancers' momentary movement.

You will need
- [ ] a drawing board
- [ ] A3 sheets of paper
- [ ] 2B, 4B and 6B pencils
- [ ] a dip pen, nibs and ink
- [ ] a bamboo pen
- [ ] brushes
- [ ] white oil crayon
- [ ] white gouache
- [ ] charcoal
- [ ] a charcoal pencil
- [ ] a plastic eraser
- [ ] a ruler
- [ ] a sharp craft knife
- [ ] a stacking palette (cabinet nest)
- [ ] rubber-based glue
- [ ] a container of water

Mixed media line techniques

On an A3 sheet of paper mark out a rectangle measuring 37.5 × 15cm (15 × 6in.) with a pencil and ruler. Divide the rectangle into five rectangles measuring 15 × 7.5cm (6 × 3in.). Mark these boxes 1 to 5 from left to right.

1 Draw a series of lines the length of the box alternating between pen and brush. Make the lines of different widths and draw them in one movement; do not worry about how straight they are. Using your waxed crayon, zig-zag a line across the width of the box, dragging the still-wet ink as you go.

2 Starting at the top of the box make a looped line in 4B pencil that runs to the bottom. Using charcoal pencil, start to create a spiral effect by overlapping the pencil lines as you loop to the bottom of the page. Do the same with stick charcoal and brush and ink.

3 Draw an oval in charcoal pencil that is approximately the length of the box. Draw a continuous pencil line in a random manner looping and zig-zagging through the oval. With the dip pen, draw a series of tight, thin lines in your pencil loops. Using a brush, splatter or flick

ink on to the central part of the oval, first covering the other boxes with spare paper to prevent their getting spotted with ink. Finally make a few random spotted marks with your brush and bamboo pen to add contrast to the line.

4 Gently draw a series of thick lines in stick charcoal across the box. You should vary the width of line, leaving some gaps of plain white paper. Draw a series of random charcoal pencil lines with a finely sharpened charcoal pencil over the stick charcoal. Vary the width of the charcoal pencil line by changing the pressure on the point as you move across the box. Using the sharp edge of a plastic eraser, rub out a series of sharp lines across the surface of the box.

5 Using charcoal pencil, draw sharp lines all across the box with different tonal gradations. Smudge these lines together in places with your fingers. When you feel that you have a sufficient tonal range, draw over the top in dip pen. Try to make as many varied lines in dip pen as you can.

Write under each box the combination of materials you have used. This will help you later if you wish to research more line or tone mixed media techniques and experiment further with the effects you can create.

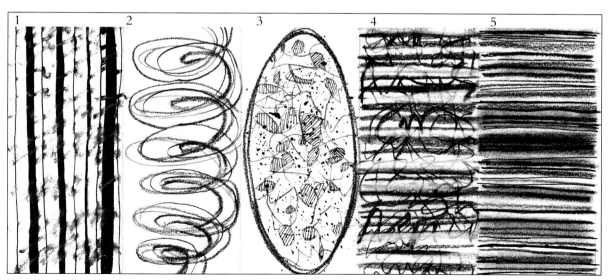

The finished exercise.

Mixed media tonal techniques

The materials for this exercise are the same as those used for the techniques in line except that a jar of water is also needed. Draw out the boxes using the same measurements as in the line techniques exercise.

With the tonal techniques a certain amount of physical pressure is needed, both in erasing vigorously and in scratching the surface of the drawing to create the slightly raised textures that appear as subtle patterns.

1 Pour a tiny amount of ink into a stacking palette, press your fingers into the ink and apply the resulting finger-prints at different strengths across the whole of the box. Then place a small object with a textured or raised surface, such as a metal food grater or a coin, under your dry finger-prints and make a series of small rubbings. Contrast the patterns created by the finger-prints with the rubbings.

2 Draw a variety of diagonal lines in oil crayon from the bottom left-hand corner to the top right-hand corner of the box. Mix Indian ink with an equal quantity of water in your palette. Apply this mid-tone wash across the whole of the box. You will see that the wax of the crayon resists the water, and that the white lines will appear against the grey of the background.

3 Starting with a stick of charcoal, and then going on to a charcoal pencil, compressed charcoal, and finally a 4B pencil, make a series of horizontal lines across the box to create a tonal sandwich. Apply each material in turn across the entire width of the box, making the width of each line the same as your drawing instrument. Leave occasional glimpses of paper beneath your lines to add contrast.

4 Make a thin layer of charcoal across the box. With a 6B pencil and a charcoal pencil draw looping pencil lines and zig-zagging charcoal lines over your charcoal layer. In oil crayon, draw a series of dense lines together at random parts of the box. On top of this mixture of line and tone, make a series of small tonal ovals in charcoal pencil and pencil.

Using a ruler make a series of sharp vertical lines 6 mm (¼in.) apart across your box. Erase every other line as much as you can, to create a contrast of tone and line.

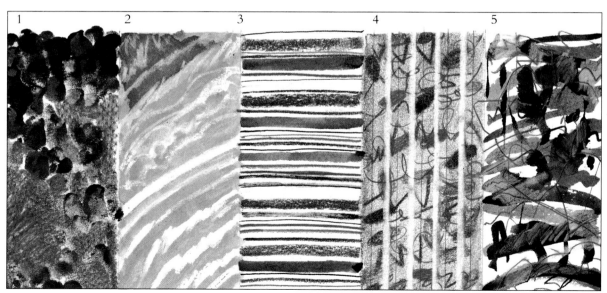

The finished exercise.

5 Draw a series of large ink lines in brush across your box. Then draw over the top of these lines in pencil even if they are still wet; be sure to press hard with your pencil. Draw another series of large ink lines across your box. Using oil crayon, try to bring out the line of the pencil against the ink, varying the pressure of the oil crayon as you rub. Finally rub out different sections of your box with an eraser to create subtle changes of pattern and texture.

Henry Moore 'Shelter Scene – Bunks and Sleepers' (detail) 480 × 426mm (19 × 17in.). Henry Moore uses a combination of varied media to create character and a sense of environment through tone.

Further ideas

To try out these techniques, you should choose different still-life subjects to draw. A section or detail of a leafy plant, a bowl of fruit, or a vase of flowers would be ideal.

Gouache resist

Divide an A3 sheet of paper into four rectangles and cut these out using a ruler and a knife. Mark out a 10cm (4in.) square in pencil in the centre of one of the rectangular sheets.

Using the white gouache, start to paint, working from the still-life subject that you have chosen. Try to vary the thickness of the lines and marks, and concentrate on the patterns within the objects and their linear quality.

When the gouache has dried completely, paint an even coat of undiluted Indian ink over the whole square. Allow that to dry.

Place the paper under a running tap, and let the gouache wash away, taking out the ink in those areas too. Rub gently with your fingers or use a soft brush until the whole image you have painted has reappeared. Place the wet paper on your drawing board to dry. You can at this stage stretch the paper (see pages 14-15) to ensure that it stays flat when it is completely dry.

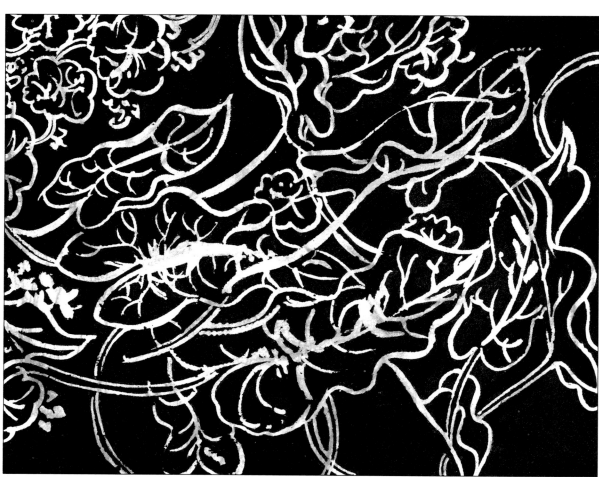

Gouache resist – a finished exercise.

Scratch technique – a finished exercise.

Glue resist – a finished exercise.

Scratch technique

Mark out a 10cm (4ins.) square in the centre of one of the prepared rectangles as described above in the gouache resist technique. To prevent the paper from buckling, you may wish to stretch the paper now (see pages 14–15). If so, allow the paper to dry before continuing with the exercise.

Paint a dense, even coat of undiluted ink over the whole square. Allow the ink to dry thoroughly.

Cover the whole square again, this time with a thick layer of white oil crayon. Go over the square several times so that it becomes completely white, and you cannot see the ink underneath. Make sure that you build up a thick layer of oil crayon as this will ensure you get very dark lines when you scratch into the surface.

Using a sharp craft knife, start to scratch away at the surface you have created. You will find that this will reveal the dark lines of the ink, in contrast to the white background. Using this scratching method, draw the image you have chosen and try to achieve the same qualities as in the gouache resist exercise, but using a very different technique.

Glue resist

Once again, mark out a 10cm (4 in.) square in the centre of a prepared rectangle. Paint the image, this time with the glue, and allow it to dry thoroughly. Pots of glue are often supplied with a brush, but you may need a thin brush to vary the thickness of the marks. It need only be a cheap brush or an old one as the glue may ruin it for other use.

When the glue has hardened, paint the square completely with an even coat of Indian ink. Once the ink has dried, rub at the surface gently with your fingers and you will find that the glue will start to peel away from the paper, revealing a clean white image.

Project: A window in mixed media

In this project I decided to do two drawings of the same window from close to and from further away, using the mixed media techniques developed in the last section. Whereas each of these could have been executed in simple tone, the interplay of line, tone and light that one gets from a window lent itself better to the more complex medium.

The first drawing was a partial view of the window. By moving my chair back a couple of metres, but still positioning it in the same relationship to the window, I could then change the focus and include the window. Both drawings started with some simple measurements, made to sight-size, of the objects in the composition. When I was satisfied with these, I then drew them in flat out. This is often a good way to start a drawing, but you have to watch out for it becoming too loose when you are drawing quickly, and be ready to make more measurements in order to reassert the structure. Measurement is a useful tool, but I find that it must not be allowed to begin to dominate the spirit of an image.

You will need
- ☐ a drawing board
- ☐ stretched A3 sheets of cartridge paper
- ☐ a 2B pencil
- ☐ a charcoal pencil
- ☐ stick charcoal
- ☐ a bamboo pen and ink
- ☐ brushes
- ☐ a white oil crayon
- ☐ a plastic eraser
- ☐ a paper stump (stomp)
- ☐ a stacking palette (cabinet nest)
- ☐ tissues
- ☐ a container of water

The finished drawing of the window (partial view).

Window – partial view

A partial view of the window set up.

Setting up

First, I stretched the sheet of cartridge paper on to my drawing board and set myself up close to the window. With the board balanced on my lap and my materials all within easy reach I focused on a small section of the window, the table, net curtains and plants.

Establishing the basic structure

Working in pencil, I made some basic sight-size measurements of the composition. To make the drawing manageable with the details clear and at the same time show most of the plant, I decided it needed to be sight-size.

I marked the section of the window frame in pencil and drew it in lightly, and then drew in the position of the plants in pencil and the lines of the net curtain in white oil crayon.

This initial stage has to be done very carefully, as a drawing whose basic structure is not properly established is difficult to get into proportion. While doing this drawing I glanced frequently from the drawing to the subject.

Filling in detail

In a light wash, and using a round-ended brush, I set about starting to fill in the shapes of the plants, window frames and net curtains. I did not

measure these lines but used the basic framework of my composition in pencil as a guide. The wash was made up as I went along, which gave me the opportunity to create some varieties in tone. I made very basic, thin washed lines to represent the net curtains.

Light tones

The lightest area in my composition was to the left of the plants where the light came in. I decided to leave this blank using the tone of the paper. The next lightest areas were the table top and net curtains where the light played on them. With an oil crayon I made bold lines and spotted marks on the areas that reflected this sensation, in the first stage of a resist technique.

Drawing the basic composition sight-size.

Laying a wash with a round-ended brush.

Using the oil crayon to create the resist surface.

Applying the wash over the oil crayon.

Applying a wash to the resist

Before applying a wash to the resist it was necessary to establish the contrasts in the composition, so I went over the darker leaves with a dark wash. When this was done I could then go over the table and curtains with a light wash, trying to make the wash reflect what I could see: light playing against the texture of the net curtain. The oil crayon repels the water of the wash, keeping these areas even lighter.

Supplying darker tones

I now felt ready to start on the darker tones. I went over the darkest areas of the side of the table and the earth in the pots with a dark wash. Using a charcoal pencil, I drew the outlines of the leaves and table edge in line, as they seemed to need emphasizing.

Final light touches

Finally, I scanned the whole of the small scene at arm's length to see what else needed doing. I decided that areas of the table top, curtains, stems and leaves were still too faint so I went over them again with a dark wash. I also felt that the curtains looked rather flat so I drew in gestural lines with the white oil crayon to give the sensation of the light shimmering against the darker shapes of the ferns.

Using a charcoal pencil to emphasize the edges.

Making gestural lines with oil crayon.

Window – full view

I moved back from my original position to give myself a good overall view of the window. This meant that I was now going to be working against the light. It was therefore even more important to establish the lightest and darkest tones in the drawing, so that the tonal proportions would be easier to attain as they fell between these extremes.

The drawing board was positioned in the same way as for the partial view drawing. When I had got this right I measured the window to sight-size as this scale seemed to fit the vertical format that I had chosen.

The framework

Using a 2B pencil for a soft line, I drew the frame of the window in lightly, making basic sight-size measurements to get the scale correct. Constantly glancing from the drawing to the subject I then scanned the plants and drew them in too. The lines of the plants are loose and flowing and had to be drawn so as not to appear rigid.

Applying darker tones

This time I elected to handle the darker areas first. The dark-toned sections of the window frame were drawn in thick charcoal, leaving the edges around it that catch the light free from charcoal.

The finished drawing.

A full view of the window set up.

Drawing the lines of the plants.

When I had finished making the tonal layer of charcoal I worked it into the paper using a paper stump (stomp) which let me achieve subtle gradations of the charcoal. I then used the plastic eraser to remove any unwanted charcoal. Next, the stump was ideal for making the lines for the plants in front of the window, providing a gentle spread of the layer of charcoal.

I created a light tonal layer of charcoal on the wall and drew in the shadow of the window frame by spreading the charcoal with the stump and erasing with the edge of a plastic eraser.

Establishing the darkest areas

At this point in the drawing I wanted to find the darkest areas. Squinting, I could see that the edges that catch the light on the window frame had the darkest lines next to them. Using brush and ink for the blackness I drew them in. The edges of the plant pot were the darkest section of the subject so I made these black using a bamboo pen.

Emphasizing light

Having done the dark areas, I then turned to the lighter ones. The net curtains were not to be shown in great detail so I drew them in a wash of ink mixed with a little water and applied with a round-ended brush. I then looked at the pots and plants and drew them in short lines using two washes, one darker than that used on the curtains.

Conveying light

Around the outside of the window the bright edges that caught the light needed sharpening, so I used a plastic eraser to make sharp lines along them. Details that did not look dark enough were filled in with charcoal. The table top was rightly the brightest part of the drawing, but the corner in reality was less bright than the rest, so I rubbed in a light layer of charcoal with the residue on a used paper stump. This also had the effect of having a crescent of light to the left of the drawing. At this point I considered the drawing finished as I had created the feeling of light entering a room.

Working the first charcoal layer.

Drawing in the darkest sections with a bamboo pen.

The net curtains put in using a round-ended brush.

Highlighting the edges with a sharpened eraser.

Further ideas

Window scenes like this make good subjects. They do not involve going outside and being exposed to the elements; you can set yourself up comfortably; there are usually several suitable objects around the window for you to draw; and you always have varied light effects. Try similar drawings, say at night or showing the view through the windows.

Window at night

Set yourself up in the same position as you used for the full view of the window. Make sure that the curtains are drawn back so that you can see the reflections in the window. If there is a reflection of yourself there, don't be modest but put it in the drawing! This time you should aim to create a drawing using mixed media that shows the relationship between the window's reflection and the window frame.

First, get the basic framework of your drawing correct by measurement, then build the major tonal relationship before you become involved with the smaller details. By combining wet and dry materials you will be able to achieve different textures and depths.

Near and far

You can also make a drawing through the window into the distance. If you would like to try the idea, you should take up the position you were in for the partial view of the window, except that you may have to be slightly higher so as to have a clear view out of the window.

A variety of mixed media materials will be necessary to do justice to the variety of the subject matter. Accurate measurement is essential to create a recession of scale and size into the background. Try using a different format of paper; for example, a thin rectangular piece. Focus on the smaller shapes in the background and show them with clarity. The objects within the room should be drawn in simple line and tone.

Project: Using a sketchbook

You will need
- a sketchbook
- 2B, 4B and 6B pencils
- a plastic eraser
- a sharp craft knife or Stanley knife

A sketchbook is your portable studio; use it whenever you do not have the time for a formal session of drawing. A sketchbook is essential for all visual artists. When you are on holiday, take it with you so that you can make studies wherever you go. The opportunities for using a sketchbook are limitless: draw out of the window of a train; draw while you are waiting in an airport lounge; draw the people you see in your local park. This will give you some practice and you will also teach yourself to observe intuitively.

Sketchbooks are available in a variety of sizes and formats; some are only pocket-sized, while others can be 60cm (2ft) wide or more. It is important to buy a sketchbook with a hardback and strong bindings that make it durable. The paper used in most sketchbooks is light cartridge; try to find one with at least this quality of paper. A sketchbook measuring about 20 × 15cm (8 × 6in.) is a convenient size.

The length of time you spend on drawings in your sketchbook should be varied. Try to make as many short studies, taking up to 2 minutes, as long ones.

You should occasionally use odd materials – ballpoint pens, fibre tips or stubby pencils; even draw with a stick dipped in ink or anything else that comes to hand. A change of materials can very often release inhibitions that have blocked your artistic development. The sketchbook is your secret world, and there is no such thing as a mistake in it.

J.M.W. Turner, detail from the sketchbook 'Hesperides I'.

Producing a study

This exercise and the following may lead you to question your own ideas on perception. They may also instinctively become a part of the way you draw. Equally, you should never be afraid to develop existing methods in creating your own drawings.

However, before embarking on more complex drawings in your sketchbook, try some experimental exercises using intuitive observation. Keep an open mind; this is a chance to be rash, to make instinctive marks, and to exaggerate the methods and techniques that you have learned.

Working from observation, make a continuous line drawing of a figure or object, keeping your

The completed study of a figure in pencil.

The basic framework.

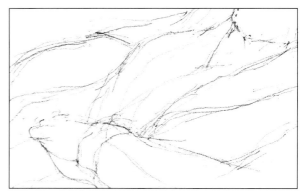

The shoulders, jacket and bed. Detail.

hand moving constantly as you look at the subject. This will help you to ensure the line is unbroken. You should try to get the proportions of the composition correct. You can use any materials you like to make the studies and vary the length of time you take.

Another good exercise is to make a series of line drawings of figures or objects. Do not look at your drawing after you have started – just look at the object and try to create the shape and line by intuition. Again you can use any materials you like, but make these studies in under a minute.

Study of a figure

A typical subject that I would want to sketch is a figure relaxing at home. People usually stay fairly still for between 15 and 30 minutes while watching television or reading. If they do make slight movements, I draw over my original lines; I frequently find this enhances the drawing, creating an animated quality. If the figure changes

position, be patient. I often have a series of positions drawn on different pages in my sketchbook. We are all creatures of habit, so a position or postures may well be repeated. If so, I can simply continue with the drawing.

I always try to look at the whole figure and in relation to its surrounding. I draw intuitively in lines of different strengths as I move around and across the shapes, constantly scanning the figure. I never measure – my sketchbook is a place for exploring instinctive marks. For this reason do not use an eraser to make changes.

Head, shoulders and pillows

The model was lying down on some pillows, watching television. I started from where the forehead and edge of the pillow met. I drew the outline of the pillow looking constantly at the subject, not at the paper. I observed the space between the pillow and the head. At first I used tentative light marks; then I worked round and across the forms. As I became more confident about the correctly plotted positions and crucial angles, I made darker marks and lines.

Shoulders, jacket and bed

I jumped from the point of the chin and marked an angle for the collar of the jacket; drawing with flowing lines the creases and folds of the jacket. I looked at the space between the figure and the outside of the bed, and drew it in outline.

54

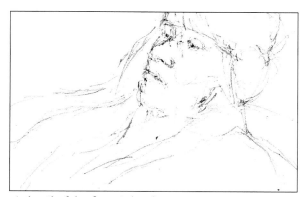

A detail of the figure's head.

The head

Then I went back to drawing the head. I looked at the proportions of the nose and cheekbones, and worked from mark to mark: lips to chin, lips to eyes, cheekbone to neck. I made tentative, light marks to indicate these points in space. As I grew more confident of the positions, I made lines and angles. As I was drawing these marks, the model changed position. The drawing was unfinished but it had been excellent practice and I could always continue with a study of a different position.

A walk with my sketchbook

Whenever I go out with my sketchbook, it is a visual adventure. One of my favourite walks takes me to the River Thames, about a mile from my home in Chiswick, London. You too may have a walk that you particularly enjoy, so you can combine this with a sketchbook project. You will be surprised what ordinary things you may have taken for granted, and how much you can enjoy drawing on your way. I decided to make six 10-minute studies on my way to the river and one of 30 minutes, when I reached my destination. I would draw objects in the local environment en route and finally a landscape. I wrote a commentary on the sketches I made as I went along; I described the last drawing – the landscape sketch – in a step-by-step sequence.

A terraced house.

Terraced house

Outside my house I made a quick drawing of my front door and balcony window. I drew the framework of the door and columns in pencil carefully. The decorative ironwork of the balcony made an intricate pattern against the window. I suggested the brickwork with horizontal lines at regular intervals. I drew the dustbins at odd angles to create a contrast with the rectangular doorway.

Bicycles against a stand.

Bicycles

I walked to the end of my road, where there was a group of bicycles propped against their stands. Standing a few paces away, I started to draw a single bicycle in relation to its stand.

I drew the frame first. Working instinctively, not using measurement, I kept the pencil on the page almost continuously. The wheels were a series of circular lines. The shape of the stand helped to give the feeling of a bicycle leaning against a stand. The essence of all sketchbook work is spontaneity, so work quickly!

Shop window

Turning off the main road and down a side street towards the river was a row of small shops. The display of fresh fish and shellfish arranged in a window was tempting. I looked at the patterns created by the different seafood and decided to draw a lobster. Flowing pencil lines seemed right for the curvaceous subject, varying the intensity and width of line. I tried to contrast the simple shape of the lobster against the rest of the fish on display around it.

Tree

At the end of the street there was a large roundabout. Struggling amidst the mass of road and cars was a number of trees. I chose one with a simple shape and drew it from the trunk towards its tapering branches, trying hard to follow the exact direction of the shape of the trunk. This was so as to capture the sense of energy rising up the tree from the ground that attracted me to it in the first place. I used light lines and marks, redrawing in heavier lines if I thought that the width or direction of the branches was wrong.

Trees are excellent linear subject matter, because their complex shape and often constant movement are difficult to draw. If you persevere and draw many of them in your sketchbook, it will enhance your skill with line.

Roof top

Then I turned down another side street and looked up at the architectural features of the houses. A chimney and part of the roof stood out against the sky. The rectangular shape of the chimney was drawn first, with the angle of the roof. I drew the chimney pots in line, trying to get their shape and convoluted outline, then quickly toned in the shape of the pots to create contrast.

Churchyard

Walking down the small, winding road I came to a churchyard and noticed a large decorative tomb. It bore an inscription: 'William Hogarth, a painter of moral tales'. Above the inscription was a charming, small stone relief. For an artist, this was irresistible. I drew it in outline, paying special attention to the overlapping features of the relief. The short study took less than 10 minutes to do.

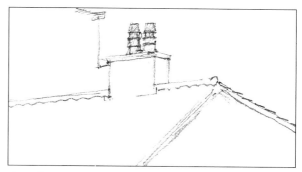

A roof top.

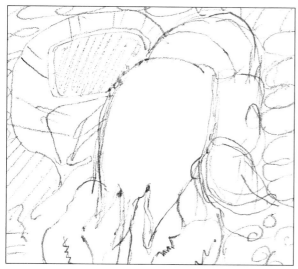

A lobster in a fishmonger's window.

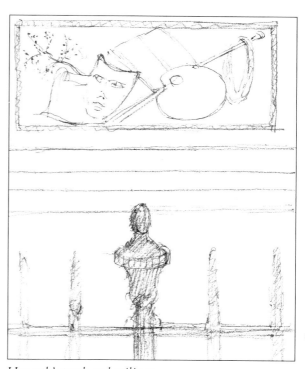

A tree against an urban landscape.

Hogarth's tomb and railings.

The river

Basic structure

Now I was at the river, I chose a subject for the longer, 30-minute sketch. Riversides are never short of interesting subject matter, so the only difficulty in selecting this barge and roadside view was the variety of choice.

Working quickly in pencil, I drew a line disecting the page in my sketchbook for the edge of the road, in front of the river. Drawing the line of the quay with the moored barge came next. The pencil moved constantly, with my eyes flicking from paper to scene rapidly.

The author drawing the river.

Fence, barge, signs and trees

Next I decided to draw the fence-posts, starting with the farthest one, as all the others would get larger as they came closer to me. Not wanting to make decisions about the tonal balance of the sketch yet, I just drew them in. The signs came next. I was trying to guess distances without measuring, jumping from point to point making marks and lines, so as to maintain the spontaneity. I varied the strength of marks when an object or angle seemed important. Lastly, I drew in the straight line for the height of the river and the edge of the boat, which meant that the basic shapes were established.

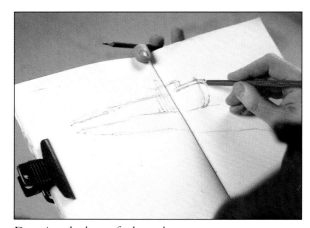

Drawing the bow of a houseboat.

The river

The afternoon light created rippled flowing lines on the surface of the river. I echoed this flow, making my pencil glide across the surface of the paper. Twisting and curling the pencil lines, I tried to create the impression of the slowly receding tide before me.

Contrast

I decided the fence-posts needed contrast against the surface of the river so I made them dark in tone. I also conveyed their haphazard placement by drawing the poles between them which were at odd angles. The surface of the road had random

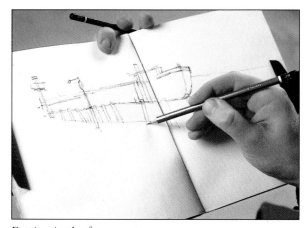

Putting in the fence-posts.

patterns; I drew these in short strokes and curved lines. I also drew in the shore and pavement.

Human scale

While I was drawing, a bearded, bohemian painter set up an easel near me and started to paint vigorously. I added his rotund outline and the line of his portable easel. The figure gave the drawing a human scale. Never be afraid to add animals or people to your pencil studies, if they appear while you are drawing; they add a spontaneous touch. One of the great problems of drawing outdoors affected me then: it began to rain so I stopped the drawing and began to walk home.

Using pencil to create contrast.

Adding another artist painting to give human scale to the drawing.

Index

Acknowledgements

Swallow Publishing wish to thank the following people and organizations for their help in preparing *Starting Drawing*. We apologize to anybody we may have omitted to mention.

The materials and equipment illustrated on pages 8-10 and 12 were kindly loaned by CJ Graphic Supplies, 35-39 Old Street, London EC1 and 2-3 Great Pulteney Street, London W1; Daler-Rowney, 12 Percy Street, London W1.

Unless indicated otherwise, all artwork is by the author.

The following individuals and organizations lent artworks: page 5 (top) Ken Howard; pages 7 (top and foot) and 40 The British Museum; pages 43 and 52 Tate Gallery, London. The work illustrated on page 43 has been reproduced by kind permission of the Henry Moore Foundation.

Thanks to Stephen Mansfield for testing the projects in this title.

Author's Acknowledgements
To Alan and Anne Thomas for use of their house, Ivan Mosely and Claire Ireland.